I0472466

CIO Business Skills

How CIOs can work effectively with the rest of the company!

"Practical, proven techniques that will help you to make your CIO career successful"

Dr. Jim Anderson

Published by:

Blue Elephant Consulting
Tampa, Florida

Printed in the United States of America

Library of Congress Control Number: 2013951699

ISBN-13: 978-1492849254

ISBN-10: 1492849251

Warning – Disclaimer

The purpose of this book is to educate and entertain. This book does not promise or guarantee that anyone following the ideas, tips, suggestions, techniques or strategies will be successful. The author, publisher and distributor(s) shall have neither liability nor responsibility to anyone with respect to any loss or damage caused, or alleged to be caused, directly or indirectly by the information contained in this book.

Acknowledgements

Any book like this one is the result of years of real-world work experience. In my over 25 years of working for 7 different firms, I have met countless fantastic people and I've been mentored by some truly exceptional ones. Although I've probably forgotten some of the people who made me the person that I am today, here is my attempt to finally give them the recognition that they so truly deserve:

- Thomas P. Anderson
- Art Puett
- Bobbi Marshall
- Bob Boggs

Dr. Jim Anderson

This book is dedicated to my wife Lori. None of this would have been possible without her love and support.

Thanks for the best 21 years of my life (so far)...!

Speaking. Negotiating. Managing. Marketing.

Table Of Contents

Why Do CIOs Need Business Skills?

What does it take to be a successful CIO? Studies have shown that the average CIO only holds on to the job for roughly 4 years – what can you do to have a longer career? It turns out that the answer to this question is simple: you need to find ways to work with the rest of the business.

What this means is that although your technical skills and your ability to work with the rest of the people in the IT department are what got you this far, it's not going to be what you need in order to stay in the job. You are going to need to develop a new set of skills.

The key to a long-term CIO career is to understand the business that your IT department exists within. There are various other departments and people that all need what your IT department has to offer, but they may not know how to ask for it. They don't speak your language.

As the CIO it's going to be your job to find ways to bridge the gap between the rest of the company and your IT department. It can be all too easy for the rest of the company to treat the IT department as a cost center and not realize the important role that you can play in making the entire organization run quicker, run smoother, and be more profitable.

The purpose of this book is to provide you with real-world examples of how a CIO can work with the rest of the business. There is no one answer to this question. Rather it requires a different way of thinking. You actually need to take the time to fully understand what the other people in the company want to accomplish and then you're going to need to find ways for the IT department to provide that.

The magic phrase that is used to describe an IT department that works well with the rest of the company is "alignment". In this book we discuss what alignment really is and we provide you with examples of how you can move your IT department closer to achieving it.

It is my hope that after having read this book you will be aware of the additional job that you've taken on as CIO – working with the rest of the business. Do this correctly and your CIO career will last a long time...!

Good luck!

- Dr. Jim Anderson, October, 2013

About The Author

I must confess that I never set out to be a CIO. When I went to school, I studied Computer Science and thought that I'd get a nice job programming and that would be that. Well, at least part of that plan worked out!

My first job was working for Boeing on their F/A-18 fighter jet program. I spent my days programming fighter jet software in assembly language and I loved it. The U.S. government decided to save some money and went looking for other countries to sell this plane to. This put me into an unfamiliar role: I started to meet with foreign military officials and I ended up having to manage groups of engineers who were working on international projects.

Time moved on and so did I. I found myself working for Siemens, the big German telecommunications company. They were making phone switches and selling them to the seven U.S. phone companies. The problem was that the switches were too complicated. Customers couldn't tell the difference between one complicated phone switch from another complicated phone switch. Once again I found myself working with the sales and marketing teams to find ways to make the great technology that the engineers had developed understandable to both internal and external customers.

I've spent over 25 years working as a senior IT professional for both big companies and startups. This has given me an opportunity to learn what it takes to manage and IT department in ways that allow it to maximize its output while becoming a valuable part of the overall company.

I now live in Tampa Florida where I spend my time managing my consulting business, Blue Elephant Consulting, teaching college courses at the University of South Florida, and traveling to work with companies like yours to share the knowledge that I have about how to create and manage successful IT departments.

I'm always available to answer questions and I can be reached at:

Dr. Jim Anderson
Blue Elephant Consulting
Email: jim@BlueElephantConsulting.com
Facebook: http://goo.gl/1TVoK
Web: http://www.BlueElephantConsulting.com/

"Unforgettable communication skills that will set your ideas free..."

Create IT Departments That Are Productive And A Valuable Asset To The Rest Of The Company !

Dr. Jim Anderson is available to provide training and coaching on the topics that are the most important to people who have to manage IT departments: how can I build a productive IT department (and keep it together) while at the same time providing the rest of the company with the IT services that they need?

 Dr. Anderson believes that in order to both learn and remember what he says, speakers need to laugh. Each one of his speeches is full of fun and humor so that what he says "sticks" with everyone.

Dr. Anderson's CIO Skills Training Includes:

1. How to identify and attract the right type of IT workers to your IT department.
2. How to build relationships with the company's senior management in order to get the support that you need?
3. How to stay on top of changing technology and security issues so that you never get surprised?

Dr. Jim Anderson works with over 100 customers per year. To invite Dr. Anderson to work with you, contact him at:

Phone: 813-418-6970 or
Email: jim@BlueElephantConsulting.com

Blue
Elephant
Consulting
Speaking.   Negotiating.   Managing.   Marketing.

Chapter 1

Alignment Sounds Like Something You Do To A Car

Alignment Sounds Like Something You Do To A Car

Ok, so everyone's been trying to fix IT departments almost since the first computers were put to work on business problems. So how come nobody has gotten it right yet? I believe that one reason that we keep missing the mark is because we really have no idea what a really good IT department looks like. We think that we know, but we really don't.

So let's figure this one out — I mean, how hard could it be? I will be the first to confess that I've spent way too much of my career viewing the IT department as something separate from the rest of the business. This comes from my belief that I knew more about how IT worked than anyone on the "business" side of the house. Give me some requirements and then go away. I'll create the best solution and will deliver it to you later on and you can thank me when you get it. I'm not sure if this ever worked, but I sure seem to think that it did a long time ago.

No matter, it sure does not work today. Instead, I believe that the role of IT has been transformed to SERVE the rest of the business. In order for this to happen, the CIO is going to have to learn to do the following four things:

1. Connect their employees' actions to the mission of the firm (sorry, I had to use the "M" word because it really is a good description). This will turn intentions into real actions.

2. Link IT and business teams and business processes together in order to truly meet the changing needs of customers.

3. Don't leave your business strategy on the shelf. Instead, constantly shape it with real-time information that you

are always receiving from your customers.

4. Create an internal culture in which all of these elements all work together — seamlessly.

Arrgh, that list looks so foreign to the way most IT departments are doing things right now that you might be tempted to say that it's impossible. Don't you dare: you are going to have to do all four of these tasks and much more in order to make sure that your firm can survive in the 21st Century.

Chapter 2

Let's Talk About IT
Trade Shows

Let's Talk About IT Trade Shows

I'm motivated to talk about trade shows this time around because I currently find myself out in Las Vegas attending the EMC World trade show. When it comes to IT trade shows, this is it — it's by, about, and for IT professionals who live, eat, and breath storage for a living.

I've worked a countless number of trade shows during my career, and unfortunately I'd have to say that most of them were a waste of time (& money!). I first came to realize this when I was working for Siemens and in preparing for THE major industry trade show. During the planning for the show the CEO said it right out loud: "This is a waste of our time, I wish that we didn't have to go. However, since we've gone once, we have to keep going or otherwise everyone will think that we've gone out of business."

Ouch! He was right — we went, we stood around and greeted folks as they walked by our booth for three days and then we went home and the world was not changed.

So if we can all agree that it's easy to do a trade show incorrectly, then how should an IT trade show be handled? As always, these reasons seem to travel in groups of three and so here are my top three suggestions for how a CIO can ensure that you'll get the most out of an IT trade show:

1. **Have a reason for going**: going to just "show the flag" is never a good idea. Instead, make sure that you have something that you are excited about that you'd like to tell the world. This might take 6 months of pre-planning in order to have a product release cycle crank out a product just before a trade show. Make sure that this "big thing" is discussed in a press release, etc. Generate your own excitement!

2. **Schedule Customer Drop Bys**: A trade show can provide a unique opportunity for your customers (or potential customers) to meet and talk with your IT product experts such as developers or product managers. This can be an invaluable opportunity to boost a customer's sense of comfort in regards to your company's products. Just hoping that a potential customer will drop by your booth is a gamble that not even Las Vegas would take.

3. **Follow up, Follow up, Follow up**: I can't tell you how many times I've worked for a company that collected customer info during the trade show and then ended up sitting on it for months after the show until it no longer had any real value. Collecting customer info these days is all done electronically and so there is no excuse for any delay in contacting the customer after the show. In fact you should plan on how you are going to contact them BEFORE you go to the show. This way you'll just have to drop the names into your system and the follow up packages will be all ready to go after you get back home.

Even in the 21st Century, trade shows play an important role in connecting industry players, customers, and partners. Plus they always generate really good stories that start *"... I was at this trade show once and..."* IT products are often complicated and can be hard to show off at a trade show so following these three suggestions can help make your participation in the next trade show an activity that really does change the world.

Chapter 3

Do We Really Need CIOs Any More?

Do We Really Need CIOs Any More?

There was an interesting article in an issue of CIO Insight that talked about the changing role of CIOs. The basic point of the story was that since today's CIOs are spending so much time (and $$$) on keeping their firms systems up and running, that they are losing their position at the strategy table.

The thinking is that if a CIO doesn't have the time to spend on thinking about where the company needs to go and how it's going to get there, then he/she doesn't need to take up space at the table where the firm's long term direction is being decided.

The article went on to point out that CIOs are being relegated to reporting to the CFO. This basically reinforces the view of the IT department as simply being a cost center. Of course there is a plus side to having a good CIO/CFO relationship; however, I think that losing access to the CEO has got to be a bad thing for both the CIO and his or her IT team.

With the arrival of cloud (aka "utility" computing), it sure looks like the CIO who is only in charge of managing existing equipment and systems will soon be no longer needed. That also means that the DBAs and other support personnel may also be at risk. Talk about change happening!

So what's a CIO (and for that matter an IT department) to do? Clearly what a CIO used to do and may be doing today is not going to cut it going forward. So what is a CIO to do?

Well, most CIOs already split their time between operations and strategy. The problem is that too many of them spend their time on the operations issues because that is what they know best — it's where they come from. Additionally, just like every IT worker out there, CIO fear having their technical skills grow dull. Where CIOs need to be spending their time is on learning where the business is going and then making sure that the IT systems are going to be there to support the firm.

We get back to that issue of alignment, but it's even more than that. CIOs need to create a way for the operations side of their job to run on autopilot — no problems, but also not requiring any time. Sounds easy, but it never is.

Chapter 4

What's More Important: Strategy, Quality, or Low Costs?

What's More Important: Strategy, Quality, or Low Costs?

Here's a challenge for you: you've just been put in charge of an IT department / branch / project because the previous person was unable to make any effective changes. What do you focus on first?

Strategy sounds very important and the business side of the house seems to spend a lot of time working on it so maybe you should also. Quality is always a crowd pleaser and that Jack Welsh over at GE sure did a lot with it. Finally, lowering costs will always make upper management smile — even if nothing else gets done at least it will be costing the company less. If you had to pick one and only one to focus on, which one would it be?

If you picked any one of these three, then you were wrong. Focusing on strategy is always fun for us IT folks because it makes everything seem like a big board game. The reality of day-to-day business is that it is performed by real people and how they work.

Thinking too much about strategy can cause us to forget this and devastate staff morale quicker than a Chinese earthquake. Leave it to IT folks to turn quality into a numbers game — you gotta love that TQM thing. What's interesting is that you can get the TQM numbers right, maybe even win the Demming Award and still not meet the needs of your internal and external customers.

Finally, lowering costs is always fun to do and generally has great short term impacts. However, experience shows that it causes the people who are actually doing the work to no longer be heard. The few IT staffers who are left after a cost lowering exercise are numb and shell shocked. So much for easy answers.

So let's think about your new challenge once again, but this time from a different vantage point. Ultimately you are not playing some sort of game that you need to win. Instead, you are trying to perform a very careful balancing act that never ends. But what are you trying to balance?

You have four different elements that need to be kept in balance: people / strategy and processes / customers. What so many CIOs and IT managers don't realize is that it's not enough to balance just one of these — that would be relatively easy. Instead, to be successful you need to balance ALL FOUR AT THE SAME TIME. Now that's hard!

Chapter 5

From Plumber To Partner: How IT Can Become Part Of A Company's Success

From Plumber To Partner: How IT Can Become Part Of A Company's Success

Current industry wisdom estimates that companies end up spending 5% – 10% of their gross revenue on all things related to Information Technology. Ouch! That means for every $1M in revenue, the IT cost could reach up to $100,000. You do the math!

In a recent article in Baseline magazine, Cary Westmark who is the VP of Technology for golf course management firm Troon Golf talked about what he's done to make IT a key part of his company's success. I liked one of his points about simply changing the vocabulary used within the IT organization. How many times this week have you heard the phrases "cost savings", "expense avoidance", "improving the bottom line" used in your department? If you haven't, then perhaps it's time to start using them.

Cary realizes that IT spending is sorta like trying to run up the down escalator: it will get you further ahead for awhile; however, your advantage will dissipate as your competitors adopt the same technology that you are using. However, the steady and continuous application of IT to real business problems can result in reductions in operating costs and can improve efficiencies. Cary goes on to revel his top 6 suggestions for making IT a vital part of the way a company does business:

1. **TCO – Live It, Love It, Learn It**: the rest of the company is always talking about Total Cost of Ownership (TCO) and IT should be doing the same. Within IT we realize that the cost of a server is not just its purchase price. Rather it's the purchase price + operating system maintenance + electricity + cooling + 3rd party software costs + etc. Some studies say that the cost of just powering a server are 3x the initial purchase price over

the life of the server. An IT device's life expectancy is roughly 3 years — after that everything starts getting much more expensive (Windows support anyone?) Having an IT plan to refresh your IT assets is the key to managing these costs.

2. **Standards Rule!**: How did Southwest airlines get to be such a successful airline? One of their main secrets is that they fly only one type of airplane — Boeing 737s. This simplifies pilot training, maintenance, ticket sales, etc. The more standardized you can keep your IT environment, the easier it becomes to manage. Standardizing also allows you to (1) reduce costs and (2) buy hardware/software in bulk and get bigger discounts. Once again, industry wisdom is that by standardizing you'll need only 1/5 the support staff that you would need to be paying for otherwise.

3. **Pull It Over Buddy** – Software License Management: This is an issue that nobody likes to talk about because we all suspect that we are probably using software that we don't have a license for. The flip side of this is that we are probably paying for licenses that we aren't using. Getting this issue under control and presenting it to the rest of the company as a cost savings program helps IT to better align with the rest of the company.

4. **To Outsource Or Not**: Welcome to the 21st Century where everyone needs to be considering how much of their IT operations they should outsource. Cary uses the following metrics to make project by project outsourcing decisions. If a job will last at least 12 months and will require more than 700 hours of effort, he hires an employee to do it. If the role is part of a strategic project (e.g. custom development) he once

again uses employees to do it. Everything else is up for outsourcing consideration.

5. **Custom vs. COTS**: Developing a customized application to support a part of your business is very much like having a baby — it signs you up for a lifetime of responsibility. Implementing large enterprise applications can be difficult and they are constantly undergoing changes. Here's a different way of looking at things: use commercial off the shelf (COTS) products and instead of changing them to fit your business, change your business to fit the products. Every time that you can do this, the savings in development and support will make the effort well worth the pain of change.

6. **Data Center or Closet?**: Where should you put your precious servers? The instinctive IT answer is to co-locate them in a data center. However, if you only have a few servers, then perhaps creating an onsite computer room will allow you to save roughly 50% what co-location would cost. Please remember: if you use a computer room, you will need to have a very good off site data backup plan.

There you have it. Six simple tips on how IT can adapt and become more of an integral part of how your company operates. Consider these just the starting point on your road to alignment success!

Chapter 6

CIO Leadership Opportunity: Learning From The Subprime Mess

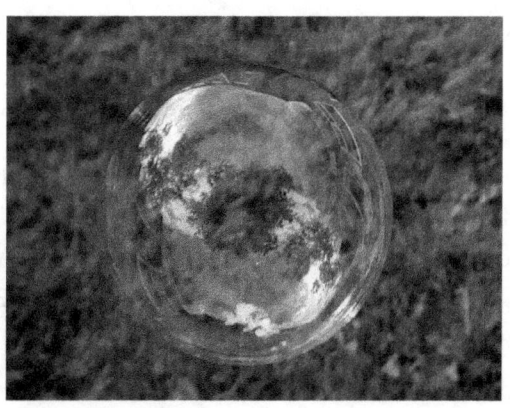

CIO Leadership Opportunity: Learning From The Subprime Mess

If you'll think back just a few years ago what we were reading in the papers and seeing on the news every day. Those folks over in the banking world got just a bit too greedy and they ended up paying the price for it. If you used the Indymac bank for your deposits, I'm hoping that you had under $100,000 in your account when the Government has had to step in and take the bank over.

As we drift along in our little Information Technology "bubble", it would be easy to look over at this rolling financial disaster and breath a sign of relief that it had nothing to do with us. But wait: that would be the wrong thing to think. This is the time for CIO's to show innovation and that that they still bring value to the company.

CIO's and their IT team can, and indeed must, use this opportunity to quickly learn what went wrong here so that we don't fall into the same trap. Errors in judgment by our CFO brethren, the inability to properly manage risk, and the failure of existing stress tests have already resulted in global bank losses of over $265 billion. IT could easily make the same mistakes (and in fact we might be doing so right now).

IT by its very nature has a great deal of risk associated with it. The subprime mess is a result of mismanagement of risk. The banks that have gotten walloped the hardest by the events that came to light ranged from Merrill Lynch to Citigroup. Each of these firms shared what is called a siloed approach to risk and compounded this problem by having poor business information communication between their risk, finance, and operations groups. Is this really all that surprising? No — attaching a high profile to risk management, whether it's in finance or IT has never been the trend.

How did this problem come about? One cause is that bankers play with investor money — not their own. Since they are betting with the bank's capital, not their own, bankers don't feel as though they have a lot of "skin in the game". If a high risk IT project goes well, then everyone gets a promotion and a larger bonus. If it fails, then it's a vendor or another department's problem.

So why does IT have the same problem? For one thing, IT splits the analysis of a project's risk up between the development team and the support team. The two sets of risk are rarely evaluated together — instead, the development issues are dealt with by one team and the operations issues by another team. Additionally, if the CIO gets behind a project, then speaking up and talking about project risk can often be a career limiting move.

So out of all of the chaos, who has handled the subprime situation correctly? Goldman was the clear winner. In December of 2006 they noticed that they were starting to see mortgage related losses. They called a meeting that included all parties involved in the mortgage business, reviewed the situation, and then Goldman started to hedge and reduce its exposure to mortgages. They still ended up taking a hit to the tune of $1.5 billion; however, they ended up doing a lot better than their competition.

What can CIO's and IT learn from both the subprime mess and Goldman's actions? First, that IT project and operations risk needs to be seen in its totality — bits and pieces can't hid in multiple departments. Secondly, don't allow the CIO to scare staff into not speaking up. Forget open door, the email system has to be wide open so that all comments and thoughts on various IT risk can be collected. Finally, when the risk of a project or operation changes, the IT department needs to come together as a whole, evaluate the changed situation, and make the correct long term decision.

Chapter 7

Here's What's Really Wrong With IT And How To Fix It

Here's What's Really Wrong With IT And How To Fix It

No holding back this time, I'm just going to let it all come out. I just got done reading my 1,000th article on how to improve an IT department and it was as worthless as most of the others that I've read.

For way too long I've been listening to gurus, consultants, and other so-called smart people who have proposed Band-Aid after Band-Aid to stop the hemorrhaging that is going on in IT right now. As an industry we seem to be going through CIO-of-the-month scenarios, my friends and colleagues are burned out and fed up, and now we're learning that the next generation of kids doesn't want to have anything to do with IT.

What's Wrong With IT?

In a nutshell, we're too different. Yeah, yeah, I know that we treasure our late start times, all night work sessions, flip-flops at the office and multi-screen desktops that sit in front of our original Star Wars posters, but it's killing us.

Foosball tables in the hallways, SQL command hierarchy charts on the wall, and action figures lined up on top of cube partitions don't do a good job of saying "we're part of this company". Instead, they say "we're different". That's the problem.

I'm not sure how this all started, but I blame air-conditioning. The early mainframe computers could only operate from within well air-conditioned rooms and so naturally the technicians who maintained and programmed them were placed in the same room or nearby. This allowed them to be hidden from the rest of the company. Out of sight, out of mind. The action figures showed up, the dress code got thrown away, and the MIS team stopped trying to fit in.

Who Cares?

You do. Your career is going to be very short and you are going to be quite bitter when your IT job goes away. The company views you and your department as a cost not an asset and they are even now looking for ways to reduce the expense that is known as you.

The CIO cares because he/she just doesn't seem to understand why none of the other executives really want to play with them. The reason is simple, the IT department is weird and so by extension the CIO must be weird and who really wants to play with a weirdo?

What To Do?

In the immortal words of the hair removal lady in the movie The 40 Year-Old Virgin, *"...this is going to hurt."* What needs to be done is that IT needs to look, act, and talk like the other parts of the company.

I'm going to go one step further and say that the role model that they need to follow is the finance department. "Ouch!" you say. Yep, put the long sleeve shirts back on, jettison the Foosball table, take down the star wars posters, and let's all get back to moving the company forward.

The thinking behind this is simple: who do we like to work with? We like to work with people who are like us. That means that if the IT department really wants to align itself with the rest of the business, then it needs to start to look like, sound like, and act like the other departments. The finance department is generally well respected and has the ear of the senior management team so they are a great role model for the IT department. In fact, the IT department should try to be viewed as finance's "brother department" — if you're talking to one, you should be talking to both.

What would this do for a CIO? First it would instantly boost his / her respectability. All of a sudden everyone would realize that the CIO and the IT department were really part of the company and that they were working to make a profit also. This would allow the CIO to start to take on different information management tasks that showed real value to the company. Finally! Alignment would be possible.

Don't get me wrong here, I like Foosball as much as the next IT staffer. However, I believe that the "IT markings" need to be taken down so that we can blend in with the rest of the company.

There should be some special place buried deep within the IT department that can be turned into a shrine for IT. This is the place where the IT employees can go to indulge in IT talk and, perhaps, play some Foosball. However, once they leave this special palace, they should re-enter a workplace that looks like they are a part of the rest of the company.

Chapter 8

IT Driving Lessons: How To Avoid A Stall

IT Driving Lessons: How To Avoid A Stall

Once upon a time in my career I had a chance to work on a fighter jet program. Talk about your ultimate IT project! During this time I learned a great deal about planes and how they work. I finally realized why during airshows a stunt airplane will often start going very fast and then pull up into a straight vertical climb – it turns out that this is very hard to do.

 If the pilot can't keep the plane going fast enough, then what you'll see is the plane start to shudder, come to a complete stop, and then the nose will pull to one side and the plane will start to hurtle towards the ground. This is all great stuff for an airshow; however, it can be disastrous for a company.

A revenue growth stall can cause even the strongest, most high flying company to come crashing down. A perfect example of this is the jeans company Levi Strauss & Company. Back in 1996 business was going gang-busters. Their sales had just popped over $7B and things were looking great. Then it stalled. By 2000 sales were only at $4.6B (down by 35%).

Not to pick on Levis Strauss. The same stall has hit Apple, Caterpillar, 3M, Toys "R" US, etc. Why should we care if we don't work for these companies? Ultimately IT needs to be the lookout that is in the crow's nest of the company and is able to detect a stall before it overtakes the company. If we are unable to do this critical job, then there is a good chance that we'll have confirmed that IT just doesn't matter anymore.

Why are stalls so deadly to a company?

Since things are going so very well just before a stall hits, many companies, just like an airplane in an air show, are actually accelerating as they enter a stall because all of the metrics that they normally use to tell them how things are going are telling them to spend, spend, spend. Senior management often never sees the stall coming.

How bad is a stall?

Some very smart guys over at the Corporate Executive Board (Matthew Olson, Derek van Bever, and Seth Verry) have done some research and what they've uncovered is that companies lose about 74% of their market capitalization (measured against the S&P 500) in the 10 years after the stall. Of course, the CEO and his/her senior team are replaced (hear that CIOs?).

Why do companies stall?

If stalls were unavoidable then there would be little for CIOs to do except to prepare defensive strategies. Research has shown that most stalls are a direct result of choices that a firm's senior management makes about either strategy or the design of the organization. What is even more damning is that 50% of the identified root causes fall into one of 4 categories:

1. Being held captive by a premium position.
2. A failure in the management of innovation within the company
3. Abandoning a core market or product too early.
4. Talent Management failures.

What's a CIO to do? We need to take a look at each of these four root causes and identify how the CIO and the IT department can make sure that the firm doesn't get stuck in a stall that all to quickly turns into a death spiral.

Chapter 9

Too Much Of A Good Thing Can Kill An IT Department

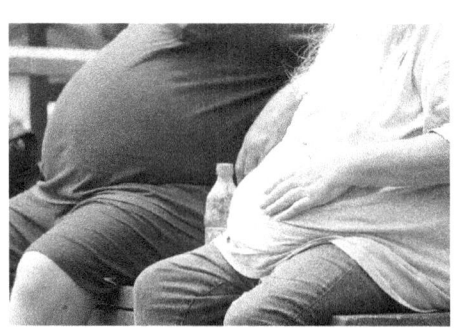

Too Much Of A Good Thing Can Kill An IT Department

If revenue is what feeds a company, then it must also be what keeps an IT department alive. Growing companies need more and more revenue to stay alive – if growth stalls, then there's a good chance that the party may be over for everyone involved (including the IT department).

But what if everything is going great? What if your firm owns the market – you are the 900 lb gorilla? Do you really have anything to worry about? Well, the answer is yes and in fact history tells us that you are probably in a sinking boat even if you don't realize it right now.

The fancy term that is used to describe 900lb market gorillas is "premium-position captivity". If you think about it, it makes sense. When you are making money hand over fist, you really don't want to do anything to rock the boat. This means that if a new, low-cost competitor shows up or if your customer suddenly changes how they value your product, you're not going to be able to react quickly enough to defend the firm. CIOs have a major role to play when this happens.

This situation is best described in the fantastic book "The Innovator's Dilemma" that if you haven't read, you really should. In the book, the hard drive business is examined and one of the points made is that 3.5" small hard drives originally had less capacity of larger hard drives so who would ever want them? Well, it turns out that small hard drives work perfectly for laptops and when that market exploded, the companies that made only the larger drives got left in the dust.

What's a CIO to do? If the senior management of a firm is unable to see impending doom, then how can a CIO possibly provide any value? The answer is simple: the CIO has access to tools and data that are not available to the rest of the firm. Awareness of the potential for a revenue stall and the will to keep a vigilant eye out for the signs can make the CIO an invaluable bellwether for the firm.

How can a CIO who works at a firm that has a dominate market position detect when a revenue stall is on the horizon? The key is for the IT department to collect and analyze market data. The data never lies. Rather, senior management who have grown accustom to seeing what they want to see discount the changes that will ultimately result in their downfall. Here is what the IT department needs to sift through the data to find:

- **Market Share Loss**: The first warning signs will be pockets of rapid market share loss. These will generally be found in specific, narrow, customer segments. It will be followed by the emergence of resistance from well-established existing customers to paying premium prices for incremental enhancements to existing products.

- **Tracking The Wrong Metrics**: More often than not, dominate firms like to track profit per customer. However, if they don't notice that customer acquisition costs have shot up, then they will end up being blindsided. Adjusting the metrics that are being tracked is key to uncovering new trends.

- **Internal Attitude**: how is the company viewing start-up competition? Is it assumed that these new players will never be able to compete with the firm for its customers? Are lower end parts of the market being turned over to them so that we can focus on the upper ends of the market with the assumption that they'll never challenge us for our part of the market?

The companies to watch today are SAP and Oracle. They are the 900 lb gorilla. Other firms such as Salesforce.com and SugarCRM have entered the market and may not be seen as a threat to the established players right now; however, time has shown that they may very well turn into tomorrow's gorillas. Let's hope that the CIOs at SAP and Oracle are already taking the correct next steps...

Chapter 10

A New CIO Job: Panning For Legal Gold

A New CIO Job: Panning For Legal Gold

One of the worst things that can happen to a modern company is to for it to get sued. Here in the 21st Century more often than not, lawsuits require that the firm being sued produce electronic documents early on in the whole messy legal process.

Good examples of how tricky this can get are the White house's attempt to retrieve firing emails, Intel's fight with AMD, and Morgan Stanley's issues with the SEC. As the Morgan Stanley case shows, if a firm can't produce the email and electronic records that are asked for it can end up costing the company a lot (US$10M in the case of Morgan Stanley). What does all of this legal stuff have to do with a CIO?

Michael Lunch is the CEO of Autonomy Corp. and he does a good job of describing how the search for electronic documents is currently done:

> **"The old-fashioned way of doing this was having a lot of lawyers doing a lot of simple things, you would literally have lawyers reading though things saying 'there was chicken for lunch.' You don't need lawyers to know that it's a lunch menu."**

Ouch – what kind of hourly rate does a firm have to pay to have lawyers read old email? This is exactly the type of situation that begs for the IT department to step in and lend a hand. Recognizing that this is an issue, the good folks at HP, Xerox, and IBM are getting ready to jump in and offer products and services.

This new reality of living in an electronic document lawsuit-happy world opens a unique door of opportunity for forward thinking CIOs. When a firm gets sued, everything has to shut down as it relates to documents while the requested material is searched for.

If an enterprising CIO had already set up a system to track and categorize the firm's electronic records, email included, then a lawsuit's requests could be easily handled. Being able to produce the requested material the next day instead of weeks or months later and being able to do it for much less than a roomful of lawyers would cost would enhance the CIO's standing among the company's senior management.

Careful – there's a right way and a wrong way to go about doing this. The wrong way is the classic IT way: I don't need anyone else, I (and my department) can do this all by ourselves. Discovery of records as a part of a legal proceeding is really the domain of the company's legal department.

This is clearly a case where the IT team needs to work WITH the legal department. Since any sort of automated search process will be taking cash out of the pockets of outside law firms who traditionally supply the human resources to do information searches, the CIO is going to need to have the full support of his in-house legal team.

The moment the lawsuit is filed, the outside firms will be whispering into the CEO's ear that he/she really needs their pricey assistance. Without the support of the in-house legal team any IT created solution will be discarded in favor of going with a "sure thing".

Having a solution in place before it is needed is the key to ensuring that the IT team looks good. If a CIO is running around after the event trying to find a solution, then expensive mistakes are going to be made. Finally we have found one area where a CIO can once and for all show the company the true value of the IT department.

Chapter 11

Fighting IT's "The Grass Is Greener" Syndrome

Fighting IT's "The Grass Is Greener" Syndrome

Businesses and IT departments can be going along just fine when all of a sudden, the business goes into what is called a "stall". Just like being in an airplane that goes into a stall, this is by no means a good thing!

When a business goes into a stall, more often than not it won't recover. The most dangerous part about a stall is that you don't see them coming – everything is fine until it isn't. There are different causes of stalls including having a premium product; however, there's another reason and the IT department plays a big role in this one.

Most companies have a small set of products or markets that they currently serve. If the company is successful, then they are probably doing a good job. The IT department has probably become optimized to support both the products and the teams that are serving these markets.

All is good. Then the *"... grass is greener on the other side of the fence..."* syndrome strikes senior management and they decide to take the company in a new direction in order to pursue more profitable markets. Of course what this means is that you need to abandon the core markets that are currently serving you so well. By doing this you won't be able to exploit any future growth that occurs in your existing markets.

Now let's be honest here, these kinds of right hand turns made by businesses rarely show up all that dramatically – at first. Instead they have a habit of sneaking in from the sides as purchases of other companies or top down mandated growth initiatives in brand new areas of business that seem to have nothing to do with the company's current customers, or products, or partners (can anyone say "Ebay buys Skype?").

If you are looking for proof that this kind of abandonment of successful markets still goes on in today's modern business environment, just open the paper and see all of the articles that are talking about public companies being bought out by private equity firms.

Clearly something went terribly wrong and outsiders had to step in. In almost every case when this kind of takeover happens, the new owners of the firm will implement a strategy for returning to what originally made the company successful and growing the core again.

Why do companies and their IT departments make these mistakes? There are two primary reasons. The first is that the company mistakenly believes that their core market(s) has become saturated. This belief is due in part to the information that the senior management is receiving from the IT department.

It's the CIO's responsibility to evaluate the data that his/her department is producing and understand what it is saying. Just because it looks like a market is all tapped out, does not necessarily mean that it is so. Instead, this is when the CIO needs to work closely with the marketing team to find different ways to measure the market.

The second cause of a firm leaving a successful market is because they feel that there are operational impediments in their core business model. This happens when senior management just despairs of being able to solve business problems that are currently confronting the company. Instead of trying to solve them, they instead decide to move to other markets which won't have the same problems.

Once again, the CIO and the IT department play a big role in this decision. There should be no business problems that the IT department can't help the rest of the company come to grips with. Whether it's tracking sales and who is buying products more closely or collecting data on how the competition is doing, the IT department can help to create solutions to almost any business problem.

Leaving a successful market is never a good idea. IT staff should be on the alert whenever they start to hear the word "mature" being used to describe the company's business situation. IT has a role to play in making sure that the company sticks with markets and customers that will serve it for a long time.

Chapter 12

What To Do When Everything That You Know Is Wrong

What To Do When Everything That You Know Is Wrong

In most IT departments, everything is fine until it isn't. Sometimes this is a result of actions that the IT department has either taken or not taken, sometimes it is a result of what's going on in the company as a whole.

No matter, everyone in IT is personally impacted when a previously successful company enters an economic stall and starts to streak towards the ground. How does an IT department end up in a situation like this and what can they do about it?

We've talked about some of reasons the companies and IT departments collude to enter a stall, things like being trapped by having a premium product, abandoning a core market segment too early, or just flat running out of good talent with which to lead the IT department.

Some of you might be thinking that such strategic matters are beyond the scope of the IT department; however, I'd disagree. IT is an information collection and distribution organization and because of this we need to be the ones who fully participate in the company's strategy discussions.

Studies done by researchers at The Executive Board, an executive think-thank, have shown that one of the leading causes of an IT department's failure to notify a company of an impending revenue stall is IT management's failure to align changes in the company's external environment to the existing company strategy. This failure rests squarely on the CIO's shoulders.

Just to drive this point home a bit more, it turns out that the assumptions that IT leadership teams have held for the longest period of time (or currently hold the most deeply), are the ones that are going to come back and bite them the hardest.

One of the reasons that this happens is because during the annual review of the company's strategic plan the CIO does not challenge the "assumptions and risk" section – he/she is willing to treat it as so much boilerplate and just let it go.

Hard work does not
guarantee success;
However, success does
not happen
without hard work.

\- Dr. Jim Anderson

Create IT Departments That Are Productive And A Valuable Asset To The Rest Of The Company !

Dr. Jim Anderson is available to provide training and coaching on the topics that are the most important to people who have to manage IT departments: how can I build a productive IT department (and keep it together) while at the same time providing the rest of the company with the IT services that they need?

Dr. Anderson believes that in order to both learn and remember what he says, speakers need to laugh. Each one of his speeches is full of fun and humor so that what he says "sticks" with everyone.

Dr. Anderson's CIO Skills Training Includes:

1. How to identify and attract the right type of IT workers to your IT department.
2. How to build relationships with the company's senior management in order to get the support that you need?
3. How to stay on top of changing technology and security issues so that you never get surprised?

Dr. Jim Anderson works with over 100 customers per year. To invite Dr. Anderson to work with you, contact him at:

Phone: 813-418-6970 or
Email: jim@BlueElephantConsulting.com

Blue
Elephant
Consulting

Speaking.   Negotiating.   Managing.   Marketing.

Photo Credits:

Cover - By: Andrea Raia
http://www.flickr.com/photos/raiadiff/

Chapter 1 - By: Steve Snodgrass
http://www.flickr.com/photos/stevensnodgrass/

Chapter 2 - By: IAVM WHQ
http://www.flickr.com/photos/iavmwhq/

Chapter 3 - By: techday.com
http://techday.com/it-brief/news/cios-optimistic-about-q2-hiring/19569/

Chapter 4 - By: Jean Synodinos
http://www.flickr.com/photos/bigscoutproject/

Chapter 5 - By: Kris
http://www.flickr.com/photos/kables/

Chapter 6 - By: Ali T
http://www.flickr.com/photos/77682540@N00/

Chapter 7 - By: Bert Palmer
http://www.flickr.com/photos/bertpalmer/

Chapter 8 - By: Anthony Roderman
http://www.flickr.com/photos/ajroder/

Chapter 9 - By: Tony Alter
http://www.flickr.com/photos/78428166@N00/

Chapter 10 - By: Flintlocker
http://www.flickr.com/photos/flintlocker/

Chapter 11 - By: I M B A
http://www.flickr.com/photos/imba_k/

Chapter 12 - By: David Goehring
http://www.flickr.com/photos/carbonnyc/

www.ingramcontent.com/pod-product-compliance
Lightning Source LLC
Chambersburg PA
CBHW071643170526
45166CB00003B/1408